The Red Beast

Controlling Anger in Children with Asperger's Syndrome

K.I. AL-GHANI

Illustrated by Haitham Al-Ghani

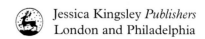

Jessica Kingsley *Publishers*
London and Philadelphia

First published in 2008
by Jessica Kingsley Publishers
73 Collier Street
London N1 9BE, UK
and
400 Market Street, Suite 400
Philadelphia, PA 19106, USA

www.jkp.com

Library of Congress Cataloging in Publication Data

Al-Ghani, K.I.
The red beast : controlling anger in children with Asperger's syndrome / K.I. Al-Ghani.
p. cm.
ISBN 978-1-84310-943-3 (pb : alk. paper)
1. Asperger's syndrome in children--Juvenile literature. 2. Anger in children--Juvenile literature. I. Title.
RJ506.A9A57 2008
618.92'858832--dc22
2008017191

British Library Cataloguing in Publication Data
A CIP catalogue record for this book is available from the British Library

ISBN 978 1 84310 943 3

Printed and bound in China

This book is dedicated to Ahmed and Sarah Al-Ghani
for their love, support and encouragement.

A word from the author

Any parent of a child with special needs will tell you that it is the uncontrollable outbursts of rage which are most difficult to contend with. Behavioural Science shows us that when a child (or adult) is angry, they simply cannot listen or be reasoned with. Adrenaline levels are so high that it makes communication almost impossible. Any attempt to placate the person just adds fuel to the fire and often results in injury and/or destruction, followed by a huge crash in self-esteem, as the anger finally abates and adrenaline levels plummet.

Over the years I have come to believe that teaching techniques, which can be used independently to control the anger, are the only way to ensure a reasonable outcome when tempers get out of control.

Some children with Autistic Spectrum Disorder (ASD) are prone to regular outbursts of rage, since simply living through a normal day is often fraught with anxiety and frustration. Children with Asperger's Syndrome seem to be the most affected because they are more self-aware. They often take any attempt to help as personal criticism and some may suffer from low self-esteem, especially when they see the results of their uncontrollable rages.

By starting early and depersonalizing the anger, it is possible to enable the child to see that anger is like a 'beast' that needs to be tamed. Taming the 'beast' can be hugely satisfying and can lead to an increase in self-esteem, not a decrease. By teaching techniques to children when they are fully in control of their tempers, role playing these visualisation techniques frequently, and then setting up a place where the children can be directed when the 'beast' awakens, it is possible to lessen the frequency and ferocity of anger and give control back to the children. The aftermath of this sort of intervention is always positive; the child can be reinforced at the earliest opportunity and self-esteem can be restored. This prevents the often destructive post-mortem many children are forced to live through once the incident is over. Questioning the child and getting them to say sorry serves no useful purpose and more often than not leads to a negative real life memory bank and the reinforcement of the very behaviour you want to change.

I have included more tried and tested strategies at the end of the book that can be used to supplement the basic visualisation techniques outlined in the story.

Deep inside everyone a Red Beast lies sleeping.

When it is asleep the Red Beast is quite small.

However, when it wakes up, it begins to grow and grow.
Strangely, as it grows, its ears begin to shrink, its eyes get
smaller and smaller and yet its mouth grows
bigger and bigger!

When fully awake, the Red Beast has tiny ears;
it can't listen!

It has tiny eyes; it can't see very well. It has a huge mouth;
it always shouts!

The Red Beast screams and calls out hurtful things like:

"I hate you!"

"Go away, leave me alone!"

The Red Beast does hurtful things like
biting, kicking, throwing, spitting and swearing!

In some people the Red Beast is very hard to wake up;
it is in a deep, deep sleep. In other people it can wake up
quickly and easily; it is only in a light sleep…

This is the story of a Red Beast that was awakened…

One bright morning a boy called Rufus was in the school playground waiting for the bell to ring. Rufus did not really like the school playground as it was always so noisy.

Suddenly someone kicked a ball and
it hit Rufus in the stomach!

Rufus was not badly hurt, but he did feel very cross and he looked around angrily to see who had kicked the ball.

The Red Beast in Rufus had woken up!
It started to grow and grow.

One of the teachers noticed the change in Rufus
and came over towards him.

"Are you all right, Rufus?" asked the teacher, kindly.

But the Red Beast had tiny ears; it couldn't listen.

John, the boy who had kicked the ball, ran over to Rufus.

"I'm really, really sorry, Rufus," he said anxiously.
However, the Red Beast had tiny eyes and it could not see
how sorry John was.

The Red Beast swore and hit out at poor John:

"I hate you! I'm gonna get you!"
it screamed with rage.

John shrank back and started to cry.

By this time, more teachers arrived.

They trapped the Red Beast and took it to a quiet place.

Red Beast **kicked** and **screamed**.

It spat at the teachers and said hurtful words.

No one looked at the beast, they just took it into
the school to the safe room.

Rufus had been in the quiet place before.

The teachers gave Rufus a stress ball.

"Try to tame the Red Beast, Rufus," they said kindly.
"You know what to do."

Rufus took a deep breath and squeezed the stress ball. Then he started to count, very slowly.

"One..., two..., three..., four..., five...," he said through gritted teeth.

Red Beast began to shrink.

"six…, seven…, eight…,
nine…, ten…,"

Red Beast felt sleepy. Its ears and eyes grew bigger,
its mouth grew smaller.

"Eleven…, twelve…, thirteen…, fourteen…, fifteen," chanted Rufus.

Red Beast grew smaller and smaller
and sleepier and sleepier.

"Sixteen..., seventeen..., eighteen..., nineteen..., twenty...,"

counted Rufus slowly as he squeezed the stress ball.

Red Beast began to snore.

One of the teachers looked in on Rufus and gave him a glass of iced water. Rufus gulped it down thirstily.

"Now Rufus, what's it to be? A foot massage and soothing music for ten minutes or a quick burst on the bubble wrap?" enquired the teacher with a wink!

"Oh, bubble wrap I think," said Rufus, sheepishly.

Rufus took a sheet of coloured bubble wrap from the 'Red Beast Box' and started popping the bubbles with relish.

After a few minutes he felt much better and was ready to go back to the classroom.

"Well done, Rufus," beamed Mrs Smith, his teacher. "You've tamed the Red Beast. Put ten beans in the class jar."

Rufus knew that when the jar was full of beans the whole class would get a special treat.

Rufus felt tired, but very proud. He noticed John looking at him from the seat near the door. Rufus **winked** at John and John **winked** back. He walked over to his table.

"I'm really sorry I hit you, John," said Rufus.

"Oh, that's okay. It wasn't you, it was the Red Beast. It's brilliant that you managed to tame him so quickly!" said John, happily.

Rufus knew that taming the beast wasn't easy and it would probably wake up again. However, now that he knew what to do, it would get easier and easier.

Other strategies

- Conduct an ABC of behaviour (Antecedent, Behaviour, Consequence) to determine if you can pinpoint any flash points, so that these can be avoided.

- Confront the child using minimal language. Do not ask questions or insist on an apology. These issues are best dealt with during circle time and certainly when the child is calm.

- Ensure the child knows where he or she can go and who to approach if they feel out of control.

- Remain calm and dispassionate at all times. You may need to practise this!

- Use soothing music and eye masks. (Sometimes covering the eyes briefly when children are engaged in aggressive situations like hair pulling can help to dispel the violence by disorientating them.)

🐾 Provide the child with foods to eat that will replenish blood sugar levels, for example grapes.

🐾 Give the child foot massages. (Often it is necessary to remove shoes in the event of kicking so this is a good way to reintroduce the shoes.)

🐾 Look at the situation during circle time, use puppets to depersonalize the event and ask the children to think up alternative solutions. You will be surprised at how the culprit often has the best ideas!

🐾 Give the child physical jobs like shredding paper, ripping up old material, popping the bubbles on bubble wrap – I love this one!

Put together a Red Beast Box that includes a stress ball, eye masks, bubble wrap, relaxation CDs, a scented pillow (lavender), small night lights to use if you like the room to be darkened during relaxation times, a bottle of still water, foods to replenish blood sugar like raisins or grapes.

 If all else fails, use the technique on yourself!

Anger Management Games for Children
Deborah M. Plummer
Illustrations by Jane Serrurier
Paperback, ISBN 978 1 84310 628 9, 160 pages

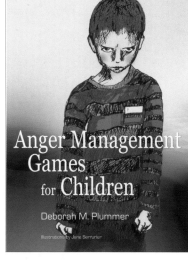

This practical handbook helps adults to understand, manage and reflect constructively on children's anger. Featuring a wealth of familiar and easy-to-learn games, it is designed to foster successful anger management strategies for children aged 5–12.

The book covers the theory behind the games in accessible language, and includes a broad range of enjoyable activities: active and passive, verbal and non-verbal, and for different sized groups. The games address issues that might arise in age-specific situations such as sharing a toy or facing peer pressure. They also encourage children to approach their emotions as a way to facilitate personal growth and healthy relationships.

This is an ideal resource for teachers, parents, carers and all those working with anger management in children.

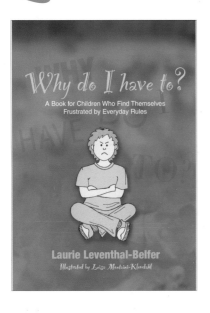

Why do I have to?
A Book for Children Who Find Themselves Frustrated by Everyday Rules
Laurie Leventhal-Belfer
Illustrated by Luisa Montaini-Klovdahl
Paperback, ISBN 978 1 84310 981 7, 80 pages

Why do I have to go to school before the show that I am watching is over? Why do I have to wear shoes and a jacket when I go outside? Rules like these can be really frustrating – but they don't have to be!

Why do I have to? looks at a set of everyday situations that provide challenges for children at home, with their friends, and at school. Laurie Leventhal-Belfer empathizes with children's wish to do things their way, explains clearly why their way does not work, and provides a list of practical suggestions for how to cope with these challenges and avoid feelings of frustration. This is the ideal book for children who have difficulty coping with the expectations of daily living, as well as for their parents and the professionals who work with them.

Caring for Myself
A Social Skills Storybook
Christy Gast and Jane Krug
Photographs by Kotoe Laackman
Hardback, ISBN 978 1 84310 872 6
Paperback, ISBN 978 1 84310 887 0
96 pages

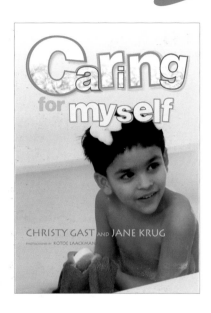

*"Hi! These are my hands. I can do many things with my hands…
When I use my hands to paint, my hands may get paint on
them. When I'm finished painting, I can wash my hands. With
clean hands, I can touch toys and furniture without getting paint
on them!"*

For a child with an autism spectrum disorder (ASD), even everyday activities like brushing your teeth, washing your hands or visiting the doctor can cause anxiety and stress because of the sensory, cognitive and communication impairments they experience.

 Caring for Myself is an entertaining and educational social skills storybook that helps children with ASDs to understand the importance of taking care of their bodies. Fully illustrated with colour photographs, it sets out fun, simple steps that explain what caring for yourself actually involves – how you can do it, where it is done and why it is important. At the end of each story is a handy 'Pause for thought' page for parents which offers tips and strategies to help a child with each activity.

 This charming book is much-loved by children with ASDs and enables them and their parents to cope with the daily activities that can be such a challenge.

Autistic Planet

Jennifer Elder

Illustrated by Marc Thomas and Jennifer Elder

Hardback, ISBN 978 1 84310 842 9, 48 pages

Autistic Planet is a magical world where all trains run exactly to time, where people working in offices have rocking chairs, and where all kids dream of winning the chess World Cup. Join us on a journey to this alternative reality, where being different is ordinary, and being "typical" is unheard of!

Full of color illustrations and written in child-friendly rhyme, this book will be much loved by children, particularly those on the autism spectrum, their parents, teachers, carers and siblings.